The Scars, Aligned

(A Cancer Narrative)

poems by

Brad Buchanan

Finishing Line Press
Georgetown, Kentucky

The Scars, Aligned

(A Cancer Narrative)

Publisher: Leah Maines
Editor: Christen Kincaid
Cover Art: Joshua Lurie-Terrell
Author Photo: Brad Buchanan, from late 2017
Cover Design: Leah Huete

Printed in the USA on acid-free paper.
Order online: www.finishinglinepress.com
            also available on amazon.com

Author inquiries and mail orders:
Finishing Line Press
P. O. Box 1626
Georgetown, Kentucky 40324
U. S. A.

Table of Contents

Foreword

When I met them, Brad Buchanan and his wife Kate Washington had already been introduced to a rare and aggressive form of T-cell lymphoma, a blood cancer threatening his career and his life. They were astute, intelligent, and anxious about their future, but the prognosis was poor. An aggressive and brutal cocktail of chemotherapy and immune therapy was required. After round three of chemo, a PET scan that images cancer (based on its hunger for glucose) was clear, but three more rounds plus an autologous stem cell transplant were still required to improve his chances for cure. As we were closing in on the completion of therapy, however, another PET scan revealed dramatic progression of his skin nodules; he was (in his own words) "lit up like a Christmas tree". Brad's only hope at this point was more chemo and a matched donor for an allogeneic transplant. Surprisingly, the chemo controlled his lymphoma and his brother was a perfect match for the transplant.

After his admission for the transplant on January 3, 2016, his home for the next three months was a 20 x 20 ft isolation room. The regime included near-lethal doses of chemotherapy and radiation to reduce the burden of cancer and allow his body to accept his brother's immune system. Engraftment occurred, and his brother's immune system traversed his body on a search and destroy mission looking for any residual cancer. Search and destroy it did. The new immune cells did not recognize the body within which they were located, and thus began Brad's Graft Versus Host Disease (GVHD). Brad experienced copious diarrhea, diffuse redness over 70% of his body, searing and maddening itching, and a painful, blinding attack on his eyes that led to tarsorrhaphy—having his eyes sown shut. Overwhelmed and confined, he drifted from a state of pain and incontinence into a near-comatose stupor. The prognosis was grim. Even the renowned GVHD expert Dr. George McDonald of the Fred Hutchinson Cancer Research Center acknowledged that for this degree of post-transplant trauma there is generally no treatment; most wither and eventually succumb.

Brad was bombarded with powerful immune suppressing medications and treated with photopheresis (a process which involved temporarily removing his blood, illuminating and taming his new immune cells and putting them back in the body). There were tubes, infusions, endless pills, intravenous feeding, and confinement day after day, week after week. Finally, after months of painstaking treatment, there were slow and incremental improvements. He faced the prospect of going home with terror: given the high level of care required, how would he survive? A boxful of pills, a bag of nutrition, weekly photopheresis sessions, an amazingly supportive and fiercely loyal wife, and Brad's own will–all assisted in his recovery. Gradually Brad got stronger, the pleasure of eating returned, and he learned to use a white cane, thus regaining some independence.

Hope seemed to be restored, but in October 2016 we observed that Epstein Barr virus-levels in his system were elevated; his suppressed immune system had allowed this virus (that most people harbor with no ill effects) to transform into a new cancer: B-cell lymphoma. Again the prognosis was very poor, but fortunately a new treatment was being developed at Memorial Sloan Kettering Hospital in New York. Enrolled in a clinical trial, Brad received white blood cells retrained specifically to attack this virus and the malignancy which it induced. In a few weeks, remission was confirmed: the virus had gone, and the PET scan was clear. After months of rehabilitation, continued medications and two corneal transplants, Brad is once again writing, riding his bike, and enjoying his family. Brad has emerged from an ordeal that makes these pages drip with emotion, expressing both the pain and the joy of his journey.

—Dr. Joseph M. Tuscano, MD. deLeuze Endowed Professor of Medicine, UC Davis Cancer Center

Author's Note

I would like to add a brief explanatory comment on the unusual nature of some of the poems included in this collection. During my innumerable medical procedures over the past 3 years or so, I often found myself silently reciting poems that I had previously memorized. This was both a tactic to distract myself from the more unpleasant aspects of what was happening to my body (I am very squeamish, a bad quality in someone who has been treated for two forms of blood cancer), and a strategy of self-calming for longer-term anxieties about life and death. This habit eventually led me attempt "Ode on a Recent Gurney," the first of the interlinear poems that appear here. This poem weaves words and phrases from John Keats's "Ode on a Grecian Urn" together with my own rather less eloquent account of my fourth biopsy, a painful procedure that spurred further reflection on my medical situation in early 2015, after I was first diagnosed with T-cell lymphoma. I wasn't quite sure what to make of this experiment, but I was intrigued (or maybe desperate) enough to repeat it with other poems, among them Wilfred Owen's "Dulce et Decorum Est," Matthew Arnold's "Dover Beach," Gerard Manley Hopkins's "Pied Beauty," and W.B. Yeats's "Byzantium." The most strenuous of these experiments, "The Fourth Quartet" mixes lines from John Milton, Dylan Thomas, and T.S. Eliot with my own words to produce something quite strange indeed.

In addition to these unusual pieces, I have also included some poems written in the style of Samuel Taylor Coleridge (whose poem on Kubla Khan I have parodied in "Glucose Scan II") and Emily Dickinson ("Vagal," and "The Outpatient's First Anniversary"). The reader will also encounter a verse narrative about the last morning I spent at home before going in for my stem cell transplant (which turned out to be a nearly four-month ordeal), written in roughly the same metrical style and stanzaic form as Wallace Stevens's meditative "Sunday Morning," whose title I have retained, with the specific date of my admission to the BMTU (Jan. 3, 2016) added.

Finally, "The Non-Complaint," the first poem I wrote after around 6 months of writer's block after my transplant (and ensuing visual impairment), was partly inspired by Edward Young's "The Complaint: or, Night-Thoughts on Life, Death, & Immortality," an eighteenth-century poem better known as "Night Thoughts." This poem, which is by no means the most eloquent or technically accomplished piece of this collection, has a special significance for me. It grew from a series of conversations during which my mother asked me whether I could write about the worst moments of my stem cell transplant; for a long time I simply refused, then eventually I summed these moments up with a three-word phrase; "crouched over darkness." In time, I managed to work these words into a poem that, unusually for me, began as a lucid dream in which I dreamt that I was composing the first few lines of the poem you will read here. When I woke up and wrote down the lines I had been dreaming (in huge print that I could barely see in the morning), I realized that they were somehow in dialogue with Young's poem, a realization that enabled me to complete the poem in due course and give it a title.

I cannot entirely explain why many my own accounts of my cancer-related experiences have been so colored by the writings of previous poets. I do not particularly care to think of my own writing as a kind of cancer growing on the body of existing poetic traditions, but I don't deny that this troubling but irresistible idea animates some of what you will read here. I suppose that one positive outcome of my time as a cancer patient is that I have learned how other poets' words not only bring meaning to what seems like pointless suffering, but can provoke new words that may, in their turn, reach others' ears. I hope that the new (and old) words in this book will reach your ears, and give you some additional strength and calm as you face whatever challenges you have to deal with.

I

Psychosomaton

my first thought bled
like reckoning
hemorrhaged, starved
then suffocated
so I kicked against
the restraints of childhood
watched the sickened
photographs of me develop
I sensed my tendons
being nibbled
grew in horror
felt so stupid
that words like "muscle"
and "vein"
seemed fragile
choking on
these jugular details
I swallowed nauseous,
nutritious spittle
fidgeted till
my tailbone rattled
down rock slides
in steep playgrounds
recovered
tasted sores
a bruise burgeoned
queasy with curiosity
heightened by
change's own
blood-vertigo
hobbled by foreign
Achilles's fortune
I joined this man's army
sprang to attention
now driven by
a fresh hypochondria's
sudden fruition
I dream diagnoses and hope
I seem human

The Differential Diagnoses

the alphabet
once scattered
throughout my blood
has metastasized
producing a poem:
"Cancer and its Early
Equivocations"
a subcutaneous
haiku sequence
individual nodules
linked mainly
by their distinctive form
perhaps only
the harmless conceit
of an overly active
imagination
but something in me
wants the capital
T-cell truth
to be spelled out
accurately at last
in all its baroque
malignancy
give me straight talk
in off-rhyme
and halting measure
or an epigram, even
with murderous
closure

My Lymphoma

you leave the thing
that kills you
your name
Lou Gehrig's disease
Achilles' tendon
our frailties frame
an identity
that we can claim
and almost believe in
funny though
that seems now
from this anonymous
distance
undiagnosed
and anomalous
still not knowing what
is wrong exactly
and how to relate
the mystery acting
inside my body
to the whole fiction
of subjectivity
that I have been
living out
I hope somehow
that it is unique
and newly discovered
in need of a breakthrough
spokesperson equipped
with a certain eloquent
fatalism
and otherwise
in decent shape

The Revelation

I have a rare form
of T-cell lymphoma
it has responded
well to treatment
in general
the main question
now is whether
the cancer
has spread into
the bone marrow
as a kind of acoustic
side effect
in a terrifyingly
poised recital
they recommend
a drug by the name
of romidepsin
virtuoso from
an obscure land
with a quirky
and pious reputation
an angel to whom
I shall extend
a gradually
more clammy palm
of welcome
intravenously
three weeks on
and one week off
for six months
then we wait
for a sign

Lymph[1]

purity
freshness
expressed as
a system
of filtration
water
in its most intimate
form
interstitial
fluid
the shadow
of blood
secret sluice
of the tissues
we never knew
we had
to worry about
or irrigate
the clear sap
running
alongside our veins
pale sibling
of that blooming
passionate wine
we thought
we could drink
until we sank
into oblivion
invisible ink
in which our fate
was also written
before
it was channeled
and forgotten

---

[1] a clear-to-white fluid made of white blood cells, especially lymphocytes, the cells that attack bacteria in the blood

The Telling

the truth of things
is in the telling
so when we sit
our children down
we may avoid certain
fatal words
only warn them
that I will feel tired
sometimes
after my medicine
for up to two days
not quite the man
they have gotten used to
ready to throw down
with mock-ferocity
even at six o'clock
in the morning
instead I will claim
a sinister gentleness
my rightful weakness
we will expect them
to understand
that this is not
the same as dying
which is another word
we won't utter
as long as they don't
ask the wrong questions
they will not
come to terms
with mortality
until it happens
and each girl reckons
with the little that
we could bear to betray

Cancer Man

my younger daughter
hails me like
a new superhero
with a name
no one in their
right mind would want
she mocks me
for my newfound power
of disappearance
my alter ego
no longer secret
my compromised
bone marrow
soon to be replaced
with a chemical
stronger than anything
she can imagine
my skeleton laced
with a negative
force field
my muscles
long hidden
at last revealed
my flabby normalcy
stripped away
as though struck
by lightning
or bitten by
a mutant animal
she laughs at me
the little villain
afraid to admit
that we're all
only human

The Accomplice

joined in bed
by my elder daughter
whose heart beats like
a cornered squirrel's
even when she is
still half-asleep
I rededicate myself
to rest
though the last dream
is gone
and the soft light
strengthens
its hold on the ceiling
it is technically morning
and I would neither
send her away
back to her own bed
nor order her
into activity
so we lie together
already survivors
of the no-longer-a-secret
secret that
she keeps and shares
with three friends
every day
till she runs out
of fears

Ode on a Recent Gurney

It happens to be the fourth biopsy that gets you
Thou still unravish'd bride of quietness
   The old-fashioned one, where they have you lie face down
   Thou foster-child of silence and slow time
And put a big needle into your pelvic bone
Sylvan historian, who canst thus express
  To get the marrow in liquid and solid form
   A flowery tale more sweetly than our rhyme
And you can't even see what they are doing
What leaf-fring'd legend haunts about thy shape
   But feel the indecent pressure and the pricking
   Of deities or mortals, or of both
     The burn that always just precedes the numbing
     In Tempe or the dales of Arcady?
   The hidden invasion, the thing that says you're suffering
   What men or gods are these? What maidens loth?
Something, though the name is slow in coming
What mad pursuit? What struggle to escape?
   Into focus, and the cure still less
   What pipes and timbrels? What wild ecstasy?

Immediate a prospect, vague and vast
Heard melodies are sweet, but those unheard
   Elusive or illusive, they need more tests
   Are sweeter; therefore, ye soft pipes, play on
To know which adjective states my case best
Not to the sensual ear, but, more endear'd
   Insurance has repurposed medicine
   Pipe to the spirit ditties of no tone:
To fit its risk-averse classifications
Fair youth, beneath the trees, thou canst not leave
   The out-of-pocket pillow smells like mothballs
   Thy song, nor ever can those trees be bare
     I bite it like a bullet all the same
     Bold Lover, never, never canst thou kiss,
My pants are loose, my shirt untucked, unbuttoned
Though winning near the goal yet, do not grieve

The grind in my midsection is between
She cannot fade, though thou hast not thy bliss
    Seven and eight on the discomfort scale
For ever wilt thou love, and she be fair!

In case anybody is wondering
Ah, happy, happy boughs! that cannot shed
    Why am I so determined to live through this
Your leaves, nor ever bid the Spring adieu
"My Cancer Journey," misnomer full of pathos?
And, happy melodist, unwearied,
    Why cheat the body of its astute mutations
For ever piping songs for ever new
Just because they cast me as their victim?
More happy love! more happy, happy love!
    What if some greater miracle were to be served
For ever warm and still to be enjoy'd
       By a refusal to fight to be saved?
For ever panting, and for ever young
But that is not an option. Breathlessly
All breathing human passion far above
    I am referred for a bronchoscopy
That leaves a heart high-sorrowful and cloy'd
       Another epic-sounding obstacle
A burning forehead, and a parching tongue.

To looking, feeling, seeming, being well.
Who are these coming to the sacrifice?
    Did I mention I have had this cough
To what green altar, O mysterious priest
For months, it seems like, and it's getting worse?
Lead'st thou that heifer lowing at the skies,
    Tuberculosis hasn't been ruled out
And all her silken flanks with garlands drest?
Now nothing is too weird to worry about
What little town by river or sea shore
    Though I was vaccinated once, in France,

Or mountain-built with peaceful citadel
That seems unlikely to make much difference
Is emptied of this folk, this pious morn?
Three ghostly scars across my upper thigh
And, little town, thy streets for evermore
A vestige of barbaric wizardry
Will silent be; and not a soul to tell
They piled us into military vans
Why thou art desolate, can e'er return.

And gave us cotton swabs to catch our cries
O Attic shape! Fair attitude! with brede
The older boys were more squeamish than us
Of marble men and maidens overwrought,
The teachers said, as though in self-defense
With forest branches and the trodden weed
Peremptory as ever, believers in
Thou, silent form, dost tease us out of thought
Corporal punishment unthinkable
As doth eternity: Cold Pastoral!
Where I was born. To know they meant no harm
When old age shall this generation waste
Is hardly any comfort. Now they aim
Thou shalt remain, in midst of other woe
Their weapons far more subtly, flatter the mind
Than ours, a friend to man, to whom thou say'st,
With something like an individual curse
Beauty is truth, truth beauty,—that is all
My fate is to believe only the worst
Ye know on earth, and all ye need to know.

Miracle

the doctors had told her
that she was infertile
when she was still
a teenager
then came a bout
of ovarian cancer
successfully treated
with hormones
and a pregnancy
out of nowhere
then another
a thriving family
unimaginable before
that killing disease
and its unexpectedly
life-giving cure
I listened dumbstruck
to her story
and wondered what
new birth
my sickness might
bring me

Offering

to lay the gift
of my disease
before those who can
rightly appraise
its rarity
I am willing to fly
some distance
at my own expense
publish more or less
vain accounts
of unflattering symptoms
in the lesser-known
non-paying journals
attend conventions
where anyone
who knows
what's good for them
will be notably absent
ghost-write
my own private
press release
call it a career
a vocation
a life

Glucose Scan I

diffuse
and innumerable
densities
beneath the skin
show sugars melting
soft tissue
thickening
overlying
the abdomen
intense nodularity
scattered foci
a hyperbolic
metabolism
dominant
with some features
of consolidation
signs of a sweet
personality
gradually
becoming grim

Glucose Scan II
Or, A Vision in a Dream. A Fragment

In Xanadu did a glucose scan
Measure FDG[2] activity,
Observe nodalities that ran
Through muscle groups and under the skin
   From the head to the proximal thigh.
So twice five scattered foci were found:
Hypermetabolic[3], suspiciously round,
And there were lesions bright on the lower chest walls
With FDG SUV[4] max of 7.3;
And here were soft tissues thickening like rubber balls,
Near the posterior sacrum, atypically.

But oh! that left pulmonary hilum[5] which hinted
At a much wider spread of the lymphoma
Than first suspected! Not wholly inconsistent,
However, with a simple but persistent
Infection characteristic of pneumonia.
And into this hilum, with ceaseless mucus heaving
As if the patient in fast thick pants were breathing
A snakelike bronchoscope was duly forced
With a general anesthetic and a burst
Of swiveling metal down the throat to witness well
The trauma and collect samples to tell.
And 'mid this new procedure there was fever,
And sweat coursed over the body like a river.
Five minutes meandering with a lazy notion
That this would be the thing that killed the patient:
Not illness but a treatment that set in motion
A deathly current formerly but latent.
And 'mid this paranoia we heard from far
Ancestral voices prophesying more

---

[2] flurodeoxyglucose—radioactive tracer used in PET (Positive Emission Tomography) scans
[3] with increased metabolic activity
[4] Standardized Uptake Values as measured by FDG
[5] root of the lung

Biopsies yet, more shadows measured
With X-rays or radio waves
Where we should hear the sickly, treasured
T-cells asking to be saved.
It was a miraculously rare disease,
The force that made such densities!

A nurse with a thermometer
In a private room I saw:
She came and took my temperature
And saw that it was normal. Fear
Was over. There was nothing to cure.
Could I revive within me
Her compassionate routine
To such a robust health t'would win me,
That with newfound discipline
I would give up drinking beer,
Smoking pot and cigarettes,
And all my friends would still be cheerful
And accept me as too careful
But amusing, all regrets
Would diminish unassisted;
I would see that my new life
Held no temptation to be resisted,
Only grace to keep me safe.

A Thanksgiving

yes
I will give this thanks
to cancer
for showing me
that something in nature
needs me to live out
its tragedy
more urgently
than I could ever
live out my own truth
in my own time
the proof comes
in these autumn colors
orange, gold,
yellow, burgundy
that leaves reach
when their trees
touch winter
exceptions to the rule
of summer
that lied to us
about lasting forever

Vagal

Refuse the suggested autocorrect
To "fatal," first of all—
Then think of the word as an active verb:
To "vagal" means to fall

Asleep from stress at the sight of blood,
Or an IV in your arm;
It really freaks the nurses out—
But does no lasting harm—

As long as you don't bang your head
Too hard against the ground,
They'll treat you with renewed respect—
And maybe atropine—

Unless somehow your pulse speeds up
To normal on its own,
In which case there's a sweet relief,
An afterlife, a dream.

The vagus nerve is the one you keep
Whenever you stay calm—
Until you find that losing it
Will bring no special shame—

Depth Perception

to sleep deeply
is to sweat profusely
four times in one night
I plummet
through the atmosphere
from cloudy cover
to tropical shower
to plunge into
the imperceptibly
approaching lagoon
of a welcome
if inexpressible dream
then wake with
a shuddering chill
bedclothes clinging
with my own moisture
I am like a bed-wetter
blaming his bladder
and perhaps
I should have known
better than to lose
control of my consciousness
and its effluvia
almost as if I'd chosen
this disease
knowing just how far down
it might take me

II

Emergency

coughing up
blood rich enough
to make the tubercular
poets jealous
I sat spitting
bright jam in a bucket
while my wife ran
three red lights
to bring me here
to the E.R.
just in time
for the crisis to pass
for my body
to bore
the important machine
to which it is now
attached
death has been
exchanged for an itch
in my arm
and the fondest wish
not to be touched

The Protestor

reenacting my hemoptisis[6]
in small, symbolic
but still shocking hiccups
taking three different antibiotics
and various painkilling narcotics
stripped of my pants and shirt
urinating in plain sight
into a plastic receptacle
refusing to leave till
I'm satisfied both that
I will not choke to death
on my own blood
and that I get the right
medicine, finally
the one recommended
months ago
by my medical team
but refused by my insurance
squatting here
staging a protest
a hemorrhage-in
as if in a contest
where the last person
to leave their bed
is offered
if not a final cure
then a means of reducing
the symptoms
controlling the damage
persuading the evil cells
to behave otherwise
my own self-serving Gandhi
propagandizing
and passive-aggressively
taking a beating

---

[6] coughing up blood

from needles and empires
full of laws and learning
that something inside me
can't help resisting

Blood Draw

they take the blood
from a tentacle
of the plastic squid
buried in my arm
a bright and sinuous
machine they manacle
to the IV tower
as they administer
medicine
the red liquid
no longer
seems like mine
when they decant it
one clear tube
into another
not my sweet and vivid
life being softly
siphoned off
just some runoff
from the current
that stirs the windmill
in my bicep
no discreet yet
threatening needle
just a vacuum
at my elbow
flushed and capped
when the samples
are full
its reaches deep
and invisible

Racing the Fever

before my fever spikes again I must
meet my new oncologist
have my PICC[7] dressing changed twice
see a primary care physician
I have never met before
get another chest X-ray done
talk to my pulmonologist
one more time about my lung
and its mysteries
change my sheets around sixteen times
according to the latest sweat arithmetic
read four goodnight stories to Lucy
with the aid of oxygen
receive a dozen IV treatments
from my wife: 6, 2, and 10 o'clock
I have three walks to take
three visitors to show around
my newly cloistered cancer life
so many pills to consume with meals
so many times to inhale, exhale
as if everything were normal
maybe even if all goes well
walk the girls three blocks to school
most of all there is the time
abstract, unknown, in between
seconds, minutes, hours
days, incalculable
until either the expected chemo
or a better course of treatment comes along
a cough is all it takes to remind us
that we don't have forever to play with
before we have to scrap all these plans
before my fever spikes again

---

[7] peripherally inserted central catheter, used for delivery of chemotherapy

Chemical Warfare

the promised
and threatened
killing cure
is no longer avoidable
after all the talk
of a surgical strike
by a single agent
scrupulous, expert
we go in the end
with the old school
scorched earth
blood and thunder
approach
risking all the usual
friendly casualties
of biological crossfire
atrocious perhaps
but at least familiar
if we fail it won't be
for lack of firepower
all starting today
with a chemical cocktail
that Molotov himself
would be proud to heave

Necrosis[8]

death-breath—
the perfect, easiest rhyme
now has literal truth
dead cells in my lungs
gave those wrenching
hacking coughs
a mephitic smell
that I blamed
on medicine
now they reek
of malignancy
the smoking
decomposing body
of my long-suspected
prenatal rival
releases this telltale
air like a rumor
of posthumous
jealousy
revolting
miscarried
only partly discharged
fetus burst in the
womb-tomb
of memory

---

[8] death of living cells or tissues

Coughing It Up

bit by bit, the nasty crap
inside my lungs
(blood, pus, mucus,
and dead cancer cells)
has got to go
and the only way
is up in a sore-ribbed hurricane
of coughing strong enough
to pick up a car and fling it
around in the air
like a boy miming
some hair-raising collision
with his toys
in a quick succession
unknown even
in Vin Diesel movies
here are pillows for seat belts
and off we go
a low, rocking motion
like shaking an engine
and then the telltale
crackling ignition
hold on while the g-forces
rocket that sputum
right up through the throat
now a missile's momentum
is burning through
my guts
and liftoff is ripping
the back of my mouth open
all for a nauseous
ejaculation
barely enough phlegm
to compare
with an oyster of pure
uranium

The Deathing

they tried their best
to doctor and nurse
and medicine me
but I cancered their ass
they familied
and friended
and neighbored
they wived
and mothered
they fathered
and daughtered
chemoed
and cathetered
I hospice-cared for them
like all the rest
they second-opinioned
and they cefepimed[9]
I only had to
mortality once
they colleagued
and survival-rated
I cemeteried them
in my defense
they never should have
experted
otherwise I might not
have last-laughed

---

[9] cefepime: an antibiotic used to treat pneumonia

An Apostrophe

through the tube in my nostrils
amidst the maze of chemicals
with long lapses
for suicidal thoughts
to take shape
I have traced many terrible
presences
though not yours
O oblivion
panic
dry hacking
shallow breathing
constipation
muscle spasms
ran like a scroll under
looped infomercials
at headache volume
but even that could not
conjure an end
to the pleasure principle
something is strong
about me
that is not me
wanting to spend
one more dollar wisely
on a money-back guarantee
imitating the sexy new friend
who has fallen so
under the spell
of this product
that there is no telling what
she may do with it
such things never
live up to their packaging
and I'm willing to bet that
you're just the same
so I will leave you thus

faceless and nameless
a legend everywhere
and nowhere to be found

Awakenings

i

if you manage to sleep
for five hours, you risk uremia[10]
so you crack the protective, drug-baked
carapace that forms from the salt
on your skin and the shapes the sheets made
when you were caught at last
by unconsciousness
every part hurts, robbed of its purpose
in staying so still, but unable
to reconnect with a deeper physical
rejuvenation
so to urinate is an emergency
where certain functions scream out instructions
but nobody else really listens or cares
they are trying to sort out where the past five hours
of unconscious cellular warfare
has left them

ii

this could be the last fun game I invent
for my children: how old men wake
disappointed to find that each new body part
is still wrinkled and raw despite
all last night's efforts
which, by the way, have just come to naught—
I could not manage the long-hoped-for shit
by now, my children have learned to detect
the false notes in optimistic speech
and to check behind
the impressive gestures
of gowns
for the bare bums
of pitiful hope

---

[10] urea in the blood

Unforgettable

you never forget
the girl who gives you
your first suppository
Danielle
left a slippery fingertip
in my rectum
I thought I'd coughed it out
but there was nothing
on the floor
and the quivering entryway
reexamined
seemed to confirm
there had been full delivery
proper intercourse
had taken place
there was relief
on both sides, I believe
but on mine a certain anxiety
about the immediate
and distant future
she left
having no
further tasks to perform
I still feared
a miscarriage
my new burden
dropping too soon

The False Gestation

this cancer
is a pregnancy
of unknown origin
and duration
confinement
labor and abortion
over and over
refractory pattern
of mindless
cellular reproduction
I piss dead drugs
and their victims
away like water
sluice conception
and its network
of slaughterhouses
beget and bugger
the decaying
energies
of a becoming
I don't want
to understand
I already have all
the fatherhood
I'd ever need
to milk and mourn
in this weakened state
or in what lies beyond

A Cancer Patient's Guide to Hockey

the blades may make them
superhuman
but they are as fallible
as surgeons
if slightly more impetuous
when it is their time
to perform
their strides sever
the IV dripping
into your veins
their decisions
become directions
before you could ever
process them
ride their incisions as long
as you can
the sheet they scar
is cool and clean
and comes back refreshed
from every infusion
luminous
even in sudden-death
overtime

Dover Beach in the Radiology Wing

The sea is calm tonight.
settle down, it's just the saline solution
The tide is full, I'm pre-medicated, the iodine
shouldn't bother me this time *the moon lies fair*
Upon the straits try not to faint
make a fist if I must on the *French coast the light*
Gleams and is gone better fess up and lie down
before I fall smack on the floor *the cliffs of England stand,*
Glimmering and vast that's better but why the delay
in checking my vitals *out in the tranquil bay.*
another test to endure, another procedure
Come to the window claustrophobic as if
in a nightmare of shrinking rooms, *sweet is the night-air!*
just breathe normally, last time they checked
my oxygen absorption levels were fine
Only, from the long line of spray
they shouldn't be leaving me here for so long
Where the sea meets the moon-blanched land
when I'm neutropenic[11] , necrotic, allergic
Listen! I need transport to come right now
it's been half an hour *you hear the grating roar*
I am vulnerable, hysterical, toxic
Of pebbles which the waves draw back, at least
could we maybe close the curtain *and fling,*
At their return she said she would come back
when she'd found help *up the high strand,*
I have no idea how long that will take
Begin, and cease, I can walk there myself
it's just down the hall *and then again begin,*
or bring me a wheelchair
With tremulous cadence slow a single person
can handle that *and bring*
The eternal note of sadness in.

I am really sorry to be such a pain
Sophocles long ago
but it's now been an hour and I am still waiting

---

[11] at higher risk for infecion

Heard it on the Aegean my immunity levels
are at an all-time low *and it brought*
Into his mind this is actually now
a threat to my health *the turbid ebb and flow*

Of human misery I'd like you to call
my doctor, any one of my doctors *we*
Find also in the sound a thought,
my oxygen tank is running out
Hearing it by this distant northern sea.
and I need it to breathe under this mask

The Sea of Faith
I do appreciate your help
Was once, too, at the full, I understand
your staff is stretched and *round earth's shore*
but a bit clearer communication
Lay like the folds of a bright girdle furled.
could easily have solved this problem
But now I only hear
before I became so upset
Its melancholy, long, it seems a shame to die
of careless neglect, after so much work
expense and care *withdrawing roar,*
Retreating to the breath
Of the night-wind will a gurney be here
soon *down the vast edges drear*
I was only brought down in this bed
And naked shingles of the world.
because I felt a little bit cold

Ah, love, let us be true
To one another! please don't let's waste this chance
to cooperate *for the world, which seems*
it's the principle I'm thinking of
To lie before us like a land of dreams,
I could be back up in my own room

So various, so beautiful, so new,
relatively safe from needles and germs
Hath really neither joy, nor love, nor light,
here's the gurney at last
Nor certitude, nor peace, this is going to happen
maybe I shouldn't have complained *nor help for pain;*
if my cell phone had been working
And we are here as on a darkling plain
maybe I could have been more patient
Swept with confused alarms of struggle and flight,
in we go, one more fucking bullet to bite
Where ignorant armies clash by night.
I wonder which poem I should recite

The Neutropenics

they tend to walk after 9PM
when they hope to find the hallways empty
and to watch themselves in the perfectly
darkened windows
neon yellow ghosts
taking their medicines out for a stroll
smuggling oxygen under their masks
to sip in secret through blood-caked nostrils
you do not need to meet their eye
they will not touch you or even risk
any of the more sanguine oaths
so if you would like to
you could unabashedly
admire the smoothness
of slow footfalls
the unearthly elegance
of filmy armor
ponder at length the garish style
they work so diligently
to preserve
through its single journey
yet come to revile

Prospective

if you only looked out
my window
or walked the long straight
passageway between
University Tower
and Davis Tower
you'd hardly suspect
a city lies round
all you see are other
hospital structures
and past them trees
you'd have to go farther
than I am supposed to
to glimpse a freeway
still gleaming like gold
at 8:00 PM
a rich vein opening up
to the mountains
perhaps
an escape
I will make again
through the huddled
hidden neighborhoods
where I don't live
like this
alone

In the Absence

in the absence
of eyelashes
I accept
sincerest wishes
for my speedy
recovery
with a baleful stare
that says I
may not survive
but refuse to die
with the appropriate
modesty
pull down
the shutters
in your own house
if you do not
wish to see
the blue flame
of my grave gaze
failing
my windows
at nightfall
will blaze away

Arturo's Comb

he left it in
our shared bathroom
its plastic teeth
like black baleen
trailing salt
and pepper seaweed
in a fixed
remorseless grin
he used it once
that I remember
it tried to devour
the handsome hair
that he left matted
and tousled
thereafter
better disheveled
than thinned out
or gone

Mourning Mr. Sharma

my roommate of four days
his soft moans
were gentle lilting
songs of pain
Ativan made him
Mozartian
but he vomited
and could not stand
they gave him methadone
at last when
there was nothing else
to be done
he spoke through a tumor
in his throat
and inflammation
in his tongue
he had to say things
many times
before anyone
could understand
he tried to speak of his
grandchildren
and life in Fiji
where he was a sportsman
a bartender
a taxi driver
and a prankster
so said his daughter
who came and sighed
and wheeled him home
they gave him less than
a year to live
he died last night
I honor him

Assuaging Dr. Sun

letting Dr. Sun
catch me crying
was not so much
a mistake as it was
inevitable
the red eyes
and the shiny nose
were symptoms
that she had to decode
on her morning rounds
I answered her questions
emotional, yes
suicidal, no
mainly glad to be alive
amid many people
whom nothing can save
in fact moved to tears
by the chance
to express
such pathetic
happiness

III

Sunday Morning
(Jan. 3, 2016)

1

The usual girlish wrangles over hair
As breakfast ends in eagerness and tears:
One daughter has a play date and rushes out,
The other's in pyjamas, and wants to help
With the dishes so there's time to play ping pong
Before I have to leave for the hospital.
I'm all packed up to go, so once the cups
And plates are put away, we go downstairs,
Where I remember the Lego mess we left
And ask her to clean it up while I convert
Our new pool table to a ping-pong court.
Soon we are rallying and talking of
Her absent little sister, whom we love
And fear, and fear still more for, as she grows
Unmanageably self-willed and well-read.

2

Why should she speak of cancer to her dad?
What is paternity if it contains
Only threatening, final, mortal things?
Shall she not learn how better to get along
With one who steals her hairbands, brushes, and combs?
Shall she not improve her wrist action on serves
And change her grip when the ball comes to her forehand?
No matter that these improvements will produce
Frustration and tantrums in the girl she beats.
She has her own life to construct, from play
And self-protection, friendship, responsible
Solitude, flirtation soon ignored,
Vanity, jokes, embarrassment, the hard
Reality of other bodies' strength
Against her charming flimsiness and smile.

3

Her dad in his own way grew up shy, like her,
But with a different physical despair:
Short and pudgy till his teenaged years,
And so afraid of anatomy he would faint
At the sight of a cow's heart brought to school
Or a graceful frog posed in formaldehyde.
A bloody nose would not stop him from fighting
Even a stronger boy on a snowy hill
Where they played "king of the mountain" much too roughly,
But take him to the doctor, speak to him
In patient tones, then hide the needle's gleam,
And he would pass out cold when the poke went in.
Did such a jealous guard spoil his own vein,
And bring the blood a contaminant: the mind?
Will she inherit a pinch of all that squirming?

4

She says "Tickle me! I want to play rhino, like with Lucy!
I'm not afraid of cancer. It's not catching.
I'm not sick either, so you don't have to worry.
Mama's not back yet. We still have time.
Oh, wait, I hear someone. It's Grandpa Ernie!"
She hugs me, and runs upstairs to let him in.
The moment for that playfulness is over
Almost before its ill-advised beginning.
Why roughhouse with a man who will be leaving
For thirty days or more to have a stem-cell
Transplant he needs to live? Survival will bring
Renewal to all those forms of affection,
Or if the worst should happen, and infection
Take me before I can embrace her again,
Let the final touch be tenderness.

5

She says, "Grandpa's tired and wants to lie down.
He got up early and the drive was long.
Maybe a few more rallies you won't get
To play more ping-pong for a long time."
That's true, I have to admit, but soon remind her
That she can ask her Grandpa for a game
When he's had a rest. "And I know Uncle James
Loves pool and ping pong too," I add. My brother,
Who is coming in a few days to be my donor,
To save my life, so we can stay together
Longer than this morning will permit,
Is like a savior who reminds us of death.
She strikes the white ball higher; I send it back
Into her puny wheelhouse. She chops down
And thwacks the ball into the net again.

6

What if our last rally should go on
For minutes, hours, all night, well past the time
Of my first radiation appointment tomorrow?
Would we two players, once barely competent,
Now tireless and expert, strive to continue?
Could one miracle of new dexterity
In her create a cure for her father's body?
No, but you'd never know that to look at her:
Her pretty eyes as focused as the laser
They use in the lab to bisect my chest,
Her quick hands stabbing right and left
Like a desperate surgeon fighting emergent
Tumors, then finding hemorrhaging everywhere.
She scoops up an errant shot, proposes one more
Chance to stave off my necessary departure.

7

It's time to go upstairs. Mama is home
And Grandpa is alert again. Malpractice
Lawyer that he is, he assures us all
That the doctors will take very good care of me.
They know their patients well, they have the best
Equipment and expertise to do the job.
I seek out Nora and we hug one more time,
Our shared sobs and soft words from earlier gone
Except in unwelcome echoes. We hold one
Another closer, her head on my chest
Where they put the still-painful catheter in.
Her round, small skull beneath my hand is dense
With plans for the next four weeks. I can't fit in
Except as a text-bearing emoticon
Or a soothing bedtime ghost over FaceTime.

8

She spends the rest of the morning in her room,
Finds clues to elaborate murder mysteries
That ten year-old girls like to solve alone
Before their friends can gather and throw doubt
On all the certainties those secrets shout.
It's cold and raining outside, so she is free
To explore her mind, and watch drops of water
Find each other and trace a new path downwards.
She has her father's patient indoor manner
And likes the crafts and pastimes that he taught her.
When it grows dark, she will not fear the weather
Though storms pass through. She will not wake her mother
But weave the thunder into lucid dreams
Where she becomes a valkyrie, a healer,
A detective, a world-class ping-pong player.

Total Body Irradiation

lit up
like a Christmas tree
that PET scan
proved me refractory
in need of more than
the usual
holiday warmth
we are shaping
to crucify
this cancer
illuminate everything
under my skin
burn the stubborn
agitators off
with an X-ray
their nativity turned
to agony
in four days
ten minutes at a time
in the hope
that anything
beyond the daily
resurrection
of the sun
is just a legend
that this perverse
messiah will die
of exposure
or heat prostration
and never be
heard from again

Chimera[12]

the boy with
different-colored eyes
and other co-morbidities
like shyness
and an indefinable weakness
in the knees
at the sight of blood
knows that his innocence
is no good
he needs to assume
the shape of a hybrid
conduct a hostile takeover
of his brother's room
get immunity
from the prying eyes
of a disease
his incredulous
mirrored face
is riddled with zits
doubtful about life
up to and including his own
a cold sore rubbing
against his teeth
his smile a painful
orthodontic fiction
his body craves
someone else's will
to go on eating
and sleeping as though
all this were normal
and worthwhile

---

[12]A person with two different types of DNA; used to describe stem cell transplant recipients.

Residue

the bed in our guest room
bears my brother's smell
when I take refuge there
from my own sweaty sheets
upstairs
I nose his molten odor
foreign and forgiving
prophetic trace
of the essential
organic redemption
he will bring me
the next time he visits
the millions of stem cells
that will slowly beckon
my body back
from death
to affliction
then to safety
reviving even
my dormant taste buds
making a new bed
for me to lie in
out of an excrescence
as normal
as shedding skin
dandruff and pheromones
on a pillow case
taking a vaccine then
perspiring on my behalf
filling a bag inside a machine
with his unconscious
resilient blameless
immunity
fully expecting
that as a result
my whole being
blankets and blood type
will change

The Gift

all my life
I have waited for this
without knowing
which one
would come first
the dangerous
suffering
that gives meaning
to everything else
or the blood-borne
generosity
of a brother
who undoes
the death
I ought to have
accepted by now
every day
a new gift
deepens the craving
there is never
enough of love
or gratitude
I will take
the worst
there is to offer
I cannot find
an alternative

Amarum et Indecorum Est

(after Wilfred Owen)

Bent double, like old beggars under sacks,
I had to slouch for them to take the shot—
Knock-kneed, coughing like hags, we cursed through sludge,
An overhead cross-section skull to knees—
Till on the haunting flares we turned our backs
So they could measure the radiation I got
And towards our distant rest began to trudge.
To launch a final attack against disease.
Men marched asleep. Many had lost their boots
Today I strip to underwear and socks
But limped on, blood-shod. All went lame; all blind;
And wedge my body into this shielded frame.
Drunk with fatigue; deaf even to the hoots
They're playing Petty; normally he rocks
Of tired, outstripped Five-Nines that dropped behind.
But not this morning, not in this basement room.
Gas! Gas! Quick, boys!—An ecstasy of fumbling,
They need me to hold still for measurements
Fitting the clumsy helmets just in time;
They have to place the lung blocks perfectly
But someone still was yelling out and stumbling,
My cramping muscles force me into dance
And flound'ring like a man in fire or lime. . .
That is a silent and invisible agony
Dim, through the misty panes and thick green light,
I see the red and black marks on my chest
As under a green sea, I saw him drowning.
Where they have drawn their lines, as on a map
In all my dreams, before my helpless sight,
Their fingers poking, pushing, never rest
He plunges at me, guttering, choking, drowning.
Till they have set the locks and sealed the trap.
If in some smothering dreams you too could pace
They finally start the treatment. My head feels light
Behind the wagon that we flung him in,
As if it wished to float right out of range.

And watch the white eyes writhing in his face,
My breathing labors under this breastplate.
His hanging face, like a devil's sick of sin;
I'm sweating, and my stomach feels strange
If you could hear, at every jolt, the blood
I'm going to faint, I'm going to throw up,
Come gargling from the froth-corrupted lungs,
I'm going to say something. A word, a cry
Obscene as cancer, bitter as the cud
Would bring this tortured cure to a sudden stop
Of vile, incurable sores on innocent tongues,
But not for long. It would be worse to die
My friend, you would not tell with such high zest
Than to endure this. My prison keeps me safe
To children ardent for some desperate glory,
As, panting, wet, eyes closed, I reel upright
The old Lie; Dulce et Decorum est
And feel my sore legs under me. With relief,
Pro patria mori.
I welcome the desperate energy to fight.

My Brother's Keeper

what I shall keep of him
he will not miss
nor will he count it loss
he will come freely
to give his life
and leave
with everything he has
still in his possession
he has so much
of the precious self
I lack and need
he may dispense it
gratuitously
but I can't think the less
of his essential sacrifice
he must cross into
my disgrace
and bear its pain
however briefly
the longer anguish
may be mine
but so will
the miraculous memory

The Fourth Quartet

Do not go gentle into that good night,
There's no easy way to die at forty-five.
When I consider how my light is spent
Reading old poetry against recurrent pain
I caught the sudden look of some dead master[13]
Alive with mischief, rhyming desire with love
Old age should burn and rave at close of day,
But middle age should play it safe and sane.
Rage, rage against the dying of the light,
Outside, maybe, when I had drinks with Tim
Whom I had known, forgotten, half-recalled
Chet, Justin, Joshua, who could hold
Ere half my days in this dark world and wide,
A poem and a pint of beer in hand
Though wise men at their end know dark is right,
Happiness lies in dreaming uncontrolled
And that one talent which is death to hide
And which promotion too may mortify
Both one and many, in the brown baked features
Still melting in a savored syllable
Because their words had forked no lightning they
Were ashamed of an ambition that also
Lodg'd with me useless, though my soul more bent
To celebrate the unredeemable
The eyes of a familiar compound ghost
Self-published poet seeks a cancer
Do not go gentle into that good night.
For Pulitzer/Governor General's
To serve therewith my Maker, and present
Awards whose validation is clear:
Both intimate and unidentifiable.
How terrible a bargain to have struck
Good men, the last wave by, crying how bright
If such a thing were even possible,

---

[13] Alternating lines in this poem are quoted from Dylan Thomas's "Do Not Go Gentle into that Good Night," John Milton's Sonnet 16, and T.S. Eliot's "Little Gidding" from Four Quartets.

My true account, lest he returning chide,
Is it really nobler just to have bad luck?
So I assumed a double part, and cried,
"Why me?" Why not me? Why should I not invite
Their frail deeds might have danced in a green bay,
My soul to witness the outraged flesh's plight?
Rage, rage against the dying of the light.
There's not much left to see, or else insight
"Doth God exact day-labour, light denied?"
Poet and man had felt free from each other before
Although we were not. I was still the same
Want-ad copyist. Can't we ever get beyond that?
I fondly ask. But Patience, to prevent
C. diff[14] , counsels vanco[15] , hears the guts
That murmur, soon replies: "God doth not need
Your pain to be prolonged." People hate art,
And learn, too late, they grieved it on its way,
A mirror doubles death: mine is exhausted
And he a face still forming; yet the words sufficed
To evoke the chimera[16] : a human not manifesting
Either man's work or his own gifts: who best
Knows that two darknesses can make new light.
Do not go gentle into that good night.
An end, though natural, is violent.
Grave men, near death, who see with blinding sight
That tragic scenes could have turned out otherwise
To compel the recognition they preceded,
Anagnorisis[17] laughing. Those showing God this,
Bear his mild yoke, they serve him best. His state
Is sweeter as it seems ridiculous.
Blind eyes could blaze like meteors and be gay,
Think of Stevie Wonder carrying his head high;

---

[14] C-difficile infection
[15] vancomycin, an antibiotic
[16] an individual, organ or part consisting of tissues of diverse genetic constitution; in stem cell transplants, a patient who has received DNA from a donor
[17] moment of critical discovery

And so, compliant to the common wind
The ocean smell of heparin[18] in my mouth
Rage, rage against the dying of the light.
Castor and Pollux frozen overhead
And you, my father, there on the sad height,
Remember that another god knew death
Is kingly; thousands at his bidding speed
With doomed aplomb to their catastrophe
In concord at this intersection time
You must forgive yourself if I should die
Curse, bless, me now with your fierce tears, I pray.
(Crying helps nasal moisturization)
And post o'er land and ocean without rest:
Travel is a sincere expression of grief
Of meeting nowhere, no before and after.
Enjoy the world you gave me. You worked too hard
Do not go gentle into that good night.
Unless that space preserves a sleeping child
They also serve who only stand and wait."
You were a good, playful, attentive dad,
We trod the pavement in a dead patrol.
But you always broke the silence with a word
Rage, rage against the dying of the light.
to praise creation, even my wish to write.

---

[18] blood thinner

Out of My System

vincristine
doxorubicin
etoposide[19]
nurses handle them
with visors, gloves
and disposable gowns
before they pump
my bionic arm
full of their pink elixir
and I write their names
in the same spirit
of self-protection
I want them to get
out of my system
sooner than possible
I have already taken
those syllables
much too personally
there is nothing more
to do with them
except forget
outlive
transcend
their brutally
effective poetry
I am tired
of conjuring
with names
and nightmares
not of my choosing
whatever this is
a chapter of
be it my life or death
it is quickly closing

---

[19] drugs used in chemotherapy

Neuropath[20]

the numbing in my fingertips
and toes
marks a new limit
on what I can be
trusted to know
about knives and stoves
I no longer receive
their sharpness and heat
with the same respect
as everyone else
I am callously ignorant
of my own rightful
and needed defenses
the nervous reflex
of immediate pain
is an abstract memory
clumsy, unwittingly
vulnerable
to unnoticed incursions
of real pins and needles
not their imitations
my identity
has been jarred
slightly loose
at its roots
in my brain
where the once-
cringing neurons
now strut
unconfined

[20] person suffering from neuropathy, a disease of nerve endings

My Byzantium

The unpurged images of day recede;
I try to walk till I forget them all—
The Emperor's drunken soldiery are abed;
The drugs, the tubes, the body's bloated soul—
Night resonance recedes, night-walkers' song
Miles Davis eases me to the nearest window
After great cathedral gong;
With a languid, shimmering solo:
A starlit or a moonlit dome disdains
A city's infrastructure dully shines.
All that man is,
At every step,
All mere complexities,
My feet prepare to slip.
The fury and the mire of human veins.
A stranger saves my life with wise machines.

Before me floats an image, man or shade,
I see myself reflected, masked and gowned,
Shade more than man, more image than a shade;
With cap and hairnet, pushing medicines,
For Hades' bobbin bound in mummy-cloth
Awash in robes and fluids, twenty pounds
May unwind the winding path;
Heavier than last weekend,
A mouth that has no moisture and no breath
Steaming up my glasses with a sound
Breathless mouths may summon;
I keep as quiet as I can;
I hail the superhuman;
I am a lucky man:
I call it death-in-life and life-in-death.
I feel that even cancer is my friend.

Miracle, bird or golden handiwork,
Mesna[21] and tacrolimus[22] by my side,

---

[21] drug used to reduce undesired side effects of chemotherapy
[22] immunosuppressive drug

More miracle than bird or handiwork,
Two stoic Romans coming for a ride,
Planted on the starlit golden bough,
Encased in plastic boxes on a pole,
Can like the cocks of Hades crow,
Form the standard by which I roll:
Or, by the moon embittered, scorn aloud
They flood my heart with noble chemicals
In glory of changeless metal
Offering protection
Common bird or petal
Against fatal rejection,
And all complexities of mire or blood.
Their blue faces remote and inscrutable.

At midnight on the Emperor's pavement flit
Insistent beeping from another room,
Flames that no faggot feeds, nor steel has lit,
Transmuted by the front-desk intercom
Nor storm disturbs, flames begotten of flame,
Into a spreading chime, brings a rushing nurse—
Where blood-begotten spirits come
Someone nearby is getting even worse,
And all complexities of fury leave,
Or needs a simple task performed with love,
Dying into a dance,
Or there's been some mistake,
An agony of trance,
A dormant threat is awake
An agony of flame that cannot singe a sleeve.
And will not be appeased at this remove.

Astraddle on the dolphin's mire and blood,
Tomorrow my brother's stem cells will be in.
Spirit after spirit! The smithies break the flood,
They'll leave his veins in millions, become my skin

The golden smithies of the Emperor!
And mucous membranes, enter my bones, renew
Marbles of the dancing floor
The withered marrows, bring me back to
Break bitter furies of complexity,
An afterlife I never knew was real
Those images that yet
A self I left for dead,
Fresh images beget,
Another type of blood,
That dolphin-torn, that gong-tormented sea.
A different-tasting world in which to heal.

The Emperor of Cancer

I shake and rattle
my medicines
like a disrespected
witch doctor
my blanket a royal
mantle around
my shoulders
my gown a robe
whose hem few dare
to handle
my pink skull phallic
under a cap
my veins sustained
by a double drip
the jewel on top
of my straggling staff
shaded from light
I stroll unchallenged
around the perimeter
of my disease
surveying the forces
that could compromise
my impunity
only the authorized
and well-tested poisons
may enter the warm maze
of my body
I rule out anxieties
and side effects
my disposable socks
bestriding a world
rarefied
and relaxed

Pied Bloody

Glory be to God for dappled things—
The product of combined recessive genes,
For skies of couple color as a brinded cow;
I hated the blond hair that came from nowhere,
For rose moles all in stipple upon trout that swim
Despised my pale face and its spots of brown.
Fresh firecoal chestnut falls, finches' wings;
Unmerciful to my younger brother James,
Landscape plotted and pieced—fold, fallow and plough;
Whose teeth required an orthodontist's care,
And all trades: their gear and tackle and trim.
Whose footsteps followed too closely to my own.

All things counter, original, spare, strange;
I wanted camouflage, a uniform
Whatever is fickle, freckled (who knows how?)
Miraculously fitted, debonair,
With swift, slow; sweet, sour; adazzle, dim;
So I could choose to join or be alone.
He fathers forth whose beauty is past change:
My brother has caught up, extends his arm.
Praise him.
My long-delayed conversion has begun.

IV

A Dream

the first one
in more than a month
is of sliding through
an undersea tunnel
only big enough
for my body
a tenuous gravity
carrying me
past the narrow twists
arms crossed
on my chest
a claustrophobic
trajectory
completing itself
as long as no force
can stall my descent
something awaits me
after this crossing
a safety
less slippery
every day

Holding My Breath

early morning
another CT scan
at least this time they don't need
the iodine contrast dye
Breathe in.
pain in the ass to get that needle
then sit by myself for nearly an hour
plus it always seems to take longer
in the machine
Hold your breath.
wonder why I had that reaction
not a big deal
itchy mouth dry throat
now they say I'm allergic
give me a red bracelet every time
Breathe.
how many scans now has it been
at least five or six
freaks me out every time
to enter that whirring ring
feet first like a corpse
Breathe in.
like inhaling smoke from a joint
trying not to raunch
make them start the whole thing
all over again
piss off the technician
Hold your breath.
not like last time
no impulse to cough
pneumonia's long gone
but they still want the scan
to prove it to everyone
Breathe.
why do we exhale at first
to make room for new oxygen
always a little bit of carbon dioxide

left in the lungs
Breathe in.
automated voice
more reassuring maybe
or connected to the timing
of the laser beam
frisking my insides
Hold your breath.
Christ it feels like
I've been doing
just that for the last year
and nothing else
Breathe.
well it can't hurt to verify
one more time
that I'm still cancer free
while we're at it
Breathe in.
how many more gulps
of air do I need to take
well nothing much else to do
while I'm still lying here
Hold your breath.
cling to my paused
and throbbing life
mouth closed
and eyes sewn shut
Breathe.
they tell you not to look
at the laser beam
I can't even if I wanted to
Breathe in.
eyes still blurred
and useless for weeks now
wish they could scan those
to figure out what to do
Hold your breath.

my first words when
they unzip them for good
Breathe.
probably gasps or sighs instead

Denuded

robbed of my
normal nakedness
pink, blind and derelict as
an overgrown newborn
eunuch-in-waiting
bloated and hairless
hysterical
to my children now
without a shirt on
never mind
what I look like
in the shower
hobbledehoy
with a whiff
of the grave
about me
no eyebrows left
and merkin[23] -worthy

---

[23] pubic wig

Outside

not yet ready to go home
after one hundred days
in a hospital room
with no fresh air
or tangible sunshine
I am eventually given permission
to sit outside
with a green mask on
this May afternoon
the hospital entrance
sounds like the drop-off zone
of an incredibly busy airport
people in their regular voices
toting firm if sometimes
dubious values
cars arrogating a spacious speed
I can't imagine
I ever commanded
subtle shifts in the breeze
and cloud cover
keep me breathlessly awaiting
yet more dazzling atmospherics
I have shambled into
a masterpiece
of overwhelming blurriness
and my resurfaced sunglasses
barely conceal
the tears behind them
because it is only now
after they have removed the stitches
that kept me in the dark
that I have begun to realize
after one hundred days
in a hospital room
that I am almost ready to go home

The Visitor

immune compromised
so not truly free
though left alone
for much of the day
nostalgic for the self
whose boredom
told me survival
would seem like stardom
tired of such
complexities
as I call home life
part of me tries
to reconnect with
the slow incandescence
of my former
in-patient existence
and steers my
aimless thoughts
through the campus
of the large hospital
I had been so eager
to escape
two weeks ago
when my body still dripped
with toxins
and the distant ease
of discharged
responsibilities

Wonder Drug

what they're all looking for
I have found in her
without a single
test or appointment
her patience
is not mute acceptance
her helpfulness
is not blind trust
I can't have it covered
or make a co-payment
it comes unprescribed
let alone approved
by the FDA
but without it
I could not live long
let alone recover
strength and hope
they tell me I'm making
progress despite
the lack of any
invasive procedure
somehow I am getting better
because I know at last
how much I need her

The Scars, Aligned

The place in my stomach where they put the stitches
has become the one taut place in my gut;
the old welt where my lips were cut
is self-control when my grin overreaches

itself; the smooth, sewn flap on my knee
(that once hung loose and had to be fitted
back in) solders crucial ligaments tight;
my cornea, a corpse's, can see

more clearly; my right biceps was firmed
by a PICC line; my lapsed lung, blown out
cleaves fast to my ribs; to heal is not
merely to be safe, but to be transformed.

Icarus, from the Breakfast Nook

light stays aloft
but illuminated
objects fall to us
to be known
a leaf is briefly sustained
on its slow
erratic flight
as if flaming with grace
on its way to be damned
so we come to grief
ablaze with amazement
weighed down
by the looks
of expectant mourners
and earthbound mothers
who see in their children
dimmed eyes
and the distant
reflections of suns
that desired and died
in a life-giving instant
on fire, unaware

A Second Chance at Sunlight

home but afraid
to step out in the sun
for two whole days
I now brave the glare
my bald head struck
only for a minute
by such scalding power
I feel at last the redemptive
weakness that tells me
I will someday heal

Photopheresis[24]

the invisible sun
has tightened my face
into animal
self-protectiveness
I want to be able
to brave
this beaming god
to make my way
partly blind
I squint and stumble
my sunglasses hang
like the light yoke
of rational thought
shrugged off at last
I skirt an unknown
horizon
with unnatural cunning
follow the shadow
that leads me home
I angle away
from the burning point
let flooding heat
replace my lost vision
inside
unseen
my blood
starts to brighten

---

[24] treatment of blood with photosensitizing agent

Incognito

beardless, hence
unrecognizable
I see my daughters
safely to school
tie sparkly shoelaces
and wrangle
a high pony tail
traipse across
the hectic playground
more carefully
than usual
nobody offers
a second look
concerned or otherwise
challenging
I manage to do this
normal thing
because my disguise
is effortless
the same baseball cap
I used to wear
when I would come here
every weekday
my haircut hidden
my mirror sunglasses
in place
almost as though
I had been preparing
to vanish
in plain sight today
like a ghost

Acceptance Notice

Dear Fellow Author,

I am writing to let you know that your piece,
entitled "Alpha-Beta Peripheral T-Cell Lymphoma,
Or, Cutaneous Panniculitis-Like Lymphoma"
has been accepted for publication in the modest
literary organ I have the honor to represent.
There was much debate about the awkward title
and the confusion it seemed to reflect;
some editors felt there weren't enough symptoms
at the start, though you more than made up for that
at the end, when, if anything, there was almost too much
going on for vivid imaginative description.
I will not hide from you the fear expressed by some
on our board that your poem could start a process
by its appearance that could spell the end of our magazine
but we did not feel that justified outright rejection.
We felt more human for having read your surprising
submission and we believe that what is expressed in it
justifies our journal's existence, unpleasant though it may be.
We wish sincerely that you had never sent it,
but we all agree we cannot revert to the people we were
before you pitched it up over our transom. We hired the intern
who brought it to the board's attention and are considering
changing our name. Please return the permissions form
enclosed to receive your two free contributor's copies.
We anticipate that your work will appear in every issue
beginning with winter's special contest winners' edition.
Please don't send us any more of your writing.
We do not believe we can read more than the manuscript
already before us. Thank you, however, for giving us time
to let your strange work grow on us. We can't imagine
returning to normal operations without the change
that this awareness has wrought in us, but we pray someone
takes away your pen so that you will never write again.

The Year I Had Cancer

one day we will all talk about it this way:
that was the month
when I started to wonder and decided to go to the doctor
when they were so sure it wasn't lymphoma
      and the lumps first appeared on my stomach
when my blood counts were reexamined
      in light of the internet and anecdotes
when they wanted to study the architecture
      of the nodule they cored with their special gun
when I started perspiring and coughing
      and they admitted they might have been wrong
when the insurance would not go along
      and a second opinion had to be found
when I was proud to have something so rare
      and spouted my own misguided blood
when my left lung abandoned all functions
      and made the right one heave like a hero
when I went back in for more chemo
      and found it was easier next time through
when waiting was all anyone could do
      and I shaved off my beard and hair
when my body slowly sluiced away
      the poisonous residue of naïveté
when I got the transplant they called a cure
      and I picked life right back up again
      where I had left it the year before

The Non-Complaint:
Night Thoughts of a Cancer Patient
(after Edward Young)

I don't know why happiness should be postponed.
I used to carry golf balls home by the armful.
Crouched over darkness, I did not find it profound.
A poem is a transaction that can be transformational.
The apartment I dream of might be condemned
for lack of keys, no sense of an internal
prejudice in favor of order and command.
Faced with eternal loss, I hope survival
will make up for damages sustained.
I have a wife and daughters, mostly cheerful
but realistic enough to be forewarned
that no one who loves you can be too careful
and that fancy never fully leaves the ground.

The Outpatient's First Anniversary
(after E. D.)

I was reborn a year ago—
the painful journey home
reminded me how much had died
in that eternal room—

I found that I had lost the wife
who once had called me friend—
and in her place, a nurse, for life
that stopped, but would not end—

My children, too, were new to me—
unfathered for so long
they cried at yellow eyes that blindly
flickered, like my gown—

The restless ghost who needed breakfast
brought to him became
a halting weight that strained the stairs—
one half-step at a time—

I walk unaided now, but there
in corners lurks my cane—
in case posterity should bear
my likeness once again—

The Reading

tonight I will read to you
from a book
to prove that I have
survived all this
more than the usual
intimacy of poetry
binds us here
this is the moment
when the cure
becomes official
and worthwhile
when all that silence
and darkness
sees its patience
embodied
and multiplied
you are its essence
and reward
words imprisoned
despairing
are set free
as we speak
rip
the folded pages
of my illness
open
let the wounds breathe
your trust
you don't know
how much
you were missed

Acknowledgements

I would like to express my deep appreciation, first and foremost, to my family: my wife Kate, my daughters Nora and Lucy, my parents Joe and Susan, and my brother James. I don't know how I could have survived the experiences recorded in these poems without them; each one has provided invaluable strength and support as well as love.

I also want to thank the oncology team at the U.C. Davis Center Center, especially Dr. Joseph Tuscano and Dr. Ashley Harmon, and the many nurses and care-givers who have shown amazing kindness and understanding through many difficult times. Of these many I would like to name a few: Melissa, Frank, Sara, Ayako, Lori, Chewie, and Eloisa. I also wish to express my gratitude to the friends and colleagues who read many or all of the poems included in this book and offered honest feedback: Joshua McKinney, Doug Rice, Paul O'Donnell, Robby Ching, and Terrence Moloney.

In addition, I am grateful for the help I have received from members of the Sacramento poetry workshop I have attended sporadically over the past many years, known to me as (among other things) "Friday Night Writes": Tim, Richard, Penny, Moira, Scott, Jason, Stuart, and Dan, among others, all of whom have all shared their work with me and spurred me to keep writing poems even when it seemed nearly impossible to do so.

I am also very grateful to the staff of Finishing Line Press for their professionalism, help and encouragement; the faith they have shown in this collection of poems has meant a great deal to me.

In addition, I wish to acknowledge the fact that the following poems have appeared in print before being published in this collection:

"Acceptance Notice" has been previously published in *Damfino Press*.
"Chemical Warfare" has been previously published in *EVENT*.
"The Differential Diagnoses" has been previously published in *Canadian Literature*.
"Dover Beach in the Radiology Wing" has been previously published in *QWERTY*.
"A Dream" has been previously published in *EVENT*.
"Icarus, from the Breakfast Nook" has been previously published in *The Dalhousie Review*.
"The Protestor" has been previously published in *EVENT*.
"Psychosomaton" has been previously published in *Canadian Literature*.
"The Non-Complaint" has been previously published in *The Marsh Hawk Review*.

$\mathbf{B}$rad Buchanan was born in Windsor, Ontario, Canada, and holds degrees from McGill University, the University of Toronto, and Stanford University. He taught British and Postcolonial Literature, as well as Creative Writing, at Sacramento State University until his retirement in 2016. His poetry, fiction, and scholarly articles have appeared in nearly 200 journals, among them *Canadian Literature, The Dalhousie Review, Event, The Fiddlehead, Grain, Journal of Modern Literature, The Portland Review, The Seattle Review, Twentieth-Century Literature,* and *The Wisconsin Review.* His two previously published book-length collections of poetry (*The Miracle Shirker*, Poet's Corner Press, 2005) and *Swimming the Mirror: Poems for My Daughter*, Roan Press 2009), both received *Writer's Digest* awards. He has also published two academic books: *Hanif Kureishi* (Palgrave Macmillan 2007) and *Oedipus Against Freud: Myth and the End(s) of Humanism in Twentieth-Century British Literature* (University of Toronto Press, 2010). He was diagnosed with a rare form of T-cell lymphoma in February 2015 and, after chemotherapy and radiation treatments, underwent a stem cell transplant at the U.C. Davis Medical Center in 2016. The stem-cell transplant entailed 129 days in the hospital's transplant unit, a significant loss of vision, and a lengthy recovery period at home, during which time he was diagnosed with B-cell lymphoma induced by the Epstein-Barr virus. After participating in a clinical trial at Memorial Sloan Kettering he was declared cancer-free in early 2017, and is currently still in remission. He lives in Sacramento, California with his wife and two daughters.

CPSIA information can be obtained
at www.ICGtesting.com
Printed in the USA
FSHW011532050319
56053FS